The Birds of Islay

The Birds of Islay

A Celebration in Photographs

Gordon Langsbury and Malcolm Ogilvie

Lochindaal Press

The Photographer

Gordon Langsbury, FRPS, is a professional wildlife photographer, lecturer and author who has been photographing birds for more than 40 years. In 1978, he was elected a Fellow of the Royal Photographic Society, and is currently President of the Reading Ornithological Club.

As well as visiting Islay every year since 1970, he has travelled the world in search of subjects to photograph. His pictures regularly appear in wildlife magazines, books and on television and he has won prizes in several wildlife photographic competitions. Nest photography has never interested him and so nearly all the photographs in this book are of birds away from the nest, feeding, perching, flying and just doing what birds do. He is co-author of *A Field Guide to Photographing Birds in Britain and Western Europe* (Collins 1987), and author and presenter of the RSPB video *Photographing Birds* (1996).

The Author

Malcolm Ogilvie, PhD, CIBiol, worked as a research scientist at the Wildfowl and Wetlands Trust for 25 years before moving to Islay in 1986, where he freelances as a writer and editor. He is the local bird recorder and, in addition to continuing his studies of Islay's geese, begun in the 1960s, he has worked on Islay's raptors, owls and other birds, and recorded its plants and invertebrates. He has travelled widely, especially to the arctic.

He has been an editorial board member of both *British Birds* and *Birds of the Western Palearctic* and, as well as many scientific papers, has written several books on birds, including *Wild Geese* (Poyser 1978), *Wildfowl Behaviour Guide* (Hamlyn 1994), *A Photographic Guide to the Wildfowl of the World* (New Holland 1998) and *Grebes of the World* (Bruce Coleman 2002), as well as the booklet *The Birds of Islay, when and where to find them* (Lochindaal Press 2003).

4

First published in Great Britain in 2006 by
Lochindaal Press, Glencairn, Bruichladdich, Isle of Islay, PA49 7UN, Scotland
www.lochindaalpress.co.uk

ISBN 0 9551146 0 8

Printed in Glasgow by J.Thomson Colour Printers

Front cover - Barnacle Geese, back cover - Oystercatchers

Preface

There are several reasons why people choose to take their holidays on Islay. The eight whisky distilleries attract plenty of visitors, while for others what brings them here, often many years in succession, may be the slower pace of life, uncrowded roads, long stretches of deserted sandy beaches, good food and the friendly welcome. However, as well as being renowned for its whisky and good food, Islay is also famous for its rich and varied bird life, and birdwatchers come here from far afield to see some of the island's specialities, whether breeding Choughs or wintering geese. But you do not have to be a birdwatcher to be aware of the sheer abundance of birds here, nor the way that they make their presence felt. Walk or drive around the island and there will be flocks of birds in the fields or on the lochs or sealochs. The woodlands are alive with birdsong in the summer and seabirds wheel around the cliffs or feed just offshore. The Royal Society for the Protection of Birds has three substantial reserves on the island which it manages for the great benefit of the birdlife.

While there are books which list the bird species occurring on Islay, and detail their status, there has been no book hitherto which illustrates them. It is for this reason that the two of us, a bird photographer and frequent Islay visitor and an Islay resident and ornithologist, have combined to produce this book of photographs of Islay's birds.

We have omitted most of the vagrants which have turned up on Islay only a few times, but this still leaves a total of 171 species illustrated by the photographs, covering all the 120 species which either breed regularly or occasionally, as well as all the commoner winter visitors and passage migrants. The Introduction sets the scene by describing the main habitats to be found on the island and their most important species. The photographs, rather than follow the usual taxonomic order, are divided between the four seasons.

We are grateful to those who have helped in the production of this book, especially Carol Debney for her very helpful comments on the text and Steven Hall for the map. Gordon Langsbury thanks the following for the use of their photographs: Dickie Duckett (White-tailed Eagle), David Geoghegan (Sand Martin), Ernie Janes (Lesser Redpoll), George Jackson (Corncrake), Joy Langsbury (Islay Seasons) and Roger Wilmshurst (Tree Pipit, Grasshopper Warbler and Wood Warbler). Malcolm Ogilvie is grateful to the Islay Natural History Trust for the use of their bird records when writing the captions.

Gordon Langsbury and Malcolm Ogilvie

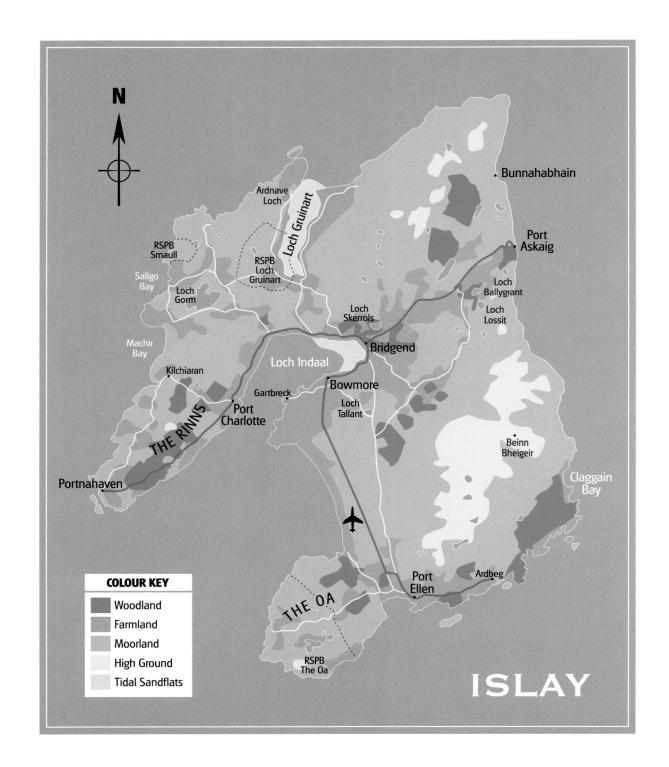

Introduction

Islay is one of the top birdwatching localities in the country. It is renowned for the tens of thousands of geese, which migrate from their Greenland breeding grounds to spend the winter, while in the summer it has up to 120 breeding species, including the great majority of the Scottish population of the Chough. Its situation at the southern end of the Inner Hebrides, off the west coast of Scotland, means that American vagrants turn up, especially in the autumn, while also at that time of year there is good seawatching for seabirds and other migrants from west coast headlands.

Islay's ornithological riches arise from a combination of its geographical position and the great variety of different habitats which it contains. Thanks to the Atlantic Ocean and the Gulf Stream, Islay has a mild climate where snow and ice are rare, with an ample, but not excessive, rainfall. This in turn has allowed areas with fertile soil to be turned into good farmland, where the grass grows almost year-round and provides the essential feeding for the flocks of geese.

Historically, Islay emerged from a kilometre-thick layer of ice about 14,000 years ago and went through a succession of tundra, scrub and finally oak forest, which probably covered most of the low ground. A wetter period around 5-7,000 years ago saw the swamping of much of the woodland by the formation of peat which gradually covered extensive areas of the lower ground. Man's arrival, probably around the same time, will have led to a further decline in tree cover and the slow conversion of the land to cropping.

In more recent times, agricultural improvements in the 18th and 19th centuries brought about the merger of many of the then very small farms into larger units, a process that has also occurred in the last 50 years. However, the 19th century also saw the abandonment of many marginal holdings on the less fertile ground, linked with the dramatic fall in the population from its peak of c.15,000 in 1931 to no more than 6,000 in the 1900s and c.3,400 today. This has left the island with extensive areas of moorland where the remains of former villages and marks of cultivation can still be found.

Woodland

In the first half of the 19th century, Islay, because of population pressure, would have had only limited areas of woodland. The first deliberate plantings were from about 1850 onwards, when new landowners began quite extensive tree planting. This was done both as an amenity and for sport, encouraging such quarry as Roe Deer and Woodcock. A third good reason for tree planting on Islay was to provide shelter from the wind, especially close to the shore where good farmland benefited by being protected from salt-laden gales.

The extensive broad-leaved woodlands around Bridgend, from Ballygrant to Dunlossit, and at Foreland and Kildalton, all date from the latter half of the 19th century and their great variety of tree species, of all ages, and good understorey make them home for many woodland species which would otherwise be absent or much scarcer. These include Wood Warbler, Treecreeper, and the various tits, as well as Blackcap and Tree Pipit. These woodlands and the many copses and shelter belts provide nest sites for Buzzard and Sparrowhawk.

The next major change to the woodland cover was the planting of conifers in the Glen, south-east of Bowmore. In their first years, they would have attracted many small birds, such as Willow and Sedge Warblers, Reed Bunting, Chaffinch, Robin and Wren. Short-eared Owls would have bred in them, too. In the 1980s and 1990s, with the trees grown up so that only the rides were negotiable, Bullfinch, Siskin, Chaffinch, and Coal Tit were common, while in 1989, several pairs of Crossbill bred following an invasion the previous autumn.

The plantations in the Glen were mostly felled around 2001 and the areas are being allowed to regenerate with hard woods. Elsewhere on the island, there was a spurt of commercial forestry planting in the 1980s, especially on the Rinns south of Port Charlotte, and also near Keills and on the Oa, about 1,800 ha in all. Like the Glen forestry, much of it was planted on wet moorland and, again like the Glen, management has usually been minimal which, combined with the exposure to gales, has meant that growth has been slow and patchy.

The use made by birds of these more recent plantings has been better recorded. Hen Harriers, in particular, adopted the plantations in their early years, finding both secure nest-sites and abundant food in the form of voles and small birds. Short-eared Owls also bred, though, as is typical of this species, in greatly varying numbers from year to year. As the trees have grown up so most of the harriers and owls have moved out, while the small bird populations have changed from species of scrub and more open habitat to those of grown trees.

The most natural woodland on the island is in the south-east, from Lagavulin eastwards to Claggain Bay; small areas of native trees, climaxing with oaks. Many of the woods have been fenced in recent years to keep out both stock and deer to allow regeneration. A similar woodland, though not entirely natural, can be found beside Loch Tallant, east of Bowmore. These woodlands contain a good mix of bird species including Islay's scarcest owl, the Tawny.

Freshwater wetlands

Fresh and salt water wetlands add hugely to Islay's attractiveness to birds. There are over 220 freshwaters of all sizes, from tiny pools on the peat (dubh lochans) to Loch Gorm, two kilometres across at its widest point. The great majority of the lochs are on peaty soils or acid rocks and support little in the way of life, whether plants, invertebrates, fish or birds. A few of the hill lochs hold breeding birds, including Red-throated Divers, as well as Teal and Mallard, and perhaps a pair of Common Sandpiper around the shore. Some of the lowland lochs are equally barren, but several are on more fertile ground and attract both breeding and wintering waterfowl.

Some of the larger lowland lochs owe their present size to dams built 100 years ago or more, as at Lochs Ballygrant, Allan and Skerrols. All three were enlarged to provide better fishing waters, while also creating heads of water for farm and domestic supply. These three lochs, together with Lochs Lossit and nan Cadhan, are among the most attractive freshwaters for birds. Breeding species on some or all of them include Little Grebe, Tufted Duck, Mallard, Teal, Moorhen and Mute Swan, while in winter they attract varying numbers of ducks, including Tufted Duck, Pochard and Goldeneye, as well as Grey Heron and the occasional Coot.

Loch Gorm, although shallow and with moderately good fertility considering it is largely surrounded by peat bogs, is disappointing for birds, largely because its size and its position on the west coast means that it is subject to considerable wave action, reducing feeding and nesting opportunities, while the low banks do not provide much shelter during gales. Small numbers of the commoner ducks can usually be seen in winter, while Mallard, Teal and Tufted Duck breed, as do the occasional pair of Red-breasted Mergansers. Loch Gorm was where Greylag Geese first bred on Islay, in 1997. Several pairs do so now and small flocks can be seen all year in the surrounding fields.

Probably the best bird loch, certainly in relation to its size, is Ardnave Loch near the mouth of Loch Gruinart. The water is shallow and also fertile, being surrounded by sandy soil, and so there are water plants and invertebrates and fish providing food for birds. Breeding birds include Mute Swan, Little Grebe, Teal and Mallard, with Redshank, Lapwing and Oystercatcher on the wet marshy area bordering the south side of the loch. In autumn, Whooper Swans often make their first stop here having flown in from Iceland, being joined by small numbers of Wigeon, Tufted Duck, Pochard and Goldeneye, all of which will stay through the winter, though the swans usually move on.

The most important wetland for birds on the island is entirely artificial. It was created by the Royal Society for the Protection of Birds on their Loch Gruinart Reserve in 1991 when they built bunds round three low-lying fields bordering the shore of Loch Gruinart and flooded them. Each of the three has its own water supply and controlled outlets to the sea so that water levels can be adjusted according to the requirements of the different seasons. The level is dropped prior to the breeding season to attract Redshank and Snipe as well as Teal and Shoveler, with higher levels in the autumn and winter which bring in up to 2,500 Teal, several hundred Wigeon and a great variety of other ducks and waders. Sitting in the hide between two of the flooded areas never disappoints and often surprises.

Much of the Loch Gruinart reserve can be regarded as a wetland. The extensive pastures of the Gruinart Flats are not only managed for grazing geese in winter, but very successfully for breeding waders in summer, with the water table controlled and wet ditches with sloping sides giving easy access to the water replacing many of the fences. This provides ideal habitat for over 200 pairs of Lapwings, together with over 100 pairs of Redshank and 60 pairs of Snipe.

Saltwater wetlands

Looking at a map of Islay shows that it is nearly cut in half by two large sealochs, Loch Gruinart in the north and the very much larger Loch Indaal in the south. Loch Gruinart is very shallow and largely dries out at low tide. The extensive sandflats at its head attract many waders, including some that stay all year, like Curlew and Oystercatcher, and others that appear on spring and, especially, autumn migration. Dunlin are much the commonest, with 3,000 or more present in late summer and autumn and up to 1,000 staying through the winter. Flocks of Knot, Sanderling and Ringed Plover are also present on migration with smaller numbers wintering. Bar-tailed Godwit are present year-round, peaking at over 300 in the winter. They are often to be found towards the mouth of the loch, as are Turnstones which feed on the rocky skerries. Also near the mouth, Great Northern Divers feed in the river channel and flocks of Eiders and Red-breasted Mergansers will spend low water, before moving up the loch with the tide.

Loch Indaal is a large sealoch, and just its inner part, which lies north and east from roughly Gartbreck across to Port Charlotte, extends to about 20 square kilometres. However, birdwatching on this seemingly very large area is made much easier by the existence of a road running right round the loch and sticking mostly very close to the shore. Admittedly, when the wind is blowing and the waves are large, finding, let alone identifying and counting, birds is quite difficult, but on calmer days, the wintering flock of 1,000-1,500 Scaup can readily be spotted in its invariable position somewhere between Bowmore and Blackrock. This is the shallowest part of the loch, little more than 2-3 metres deep, where the birds can readily dive to collect food from the bottom.

Among and around the Scaup flock, there can be up to 50 Slavonian Grebes, as well as more scattered Long-tailed Ducks and Goldeneyes. Close inshore on the Bowmore side there are beds of eelgrass, *Zostera*, on which several hundred Wigeon feed in the autumn

months, along with 30 or 40 Whooper Swans. Further down the loch, as far as Gartbreck and Port Charlotte, all three diver species occur in winter, with Great Northern the commonest, as well as up to 100 Common Scoters, and flocks of Eider Ducks and Red-breasted Mergansers. Shags and Cormorants are both present. Many divers live in the outer loch, but calm weather is needed to see them.

At the head of Loch Indaal, there is a large area of saltmarsh together with very extensive tidal sandflats. Barnacle Geese and occasionally some Greylags often feed on the saltmarsh throughout the winter, while wintering Teal and Pintail can be found in tidal pools. Shelduck feed on the sands as the tide permits, and so, too, do hundreds of Curlew and Oystercatcher, and up to 100 Bar-tailed Godwit. These three waders are present all year, while flocks of Dunlin, Sanderling and Knot are most numerous in autumn and winter. This period is also when flocks of up to 1,000 or more Golden Plover take up residence, often feeding on fields during the night and spending the daytime roosting on the sands.

Much of the coast of Islay is exposed to gales and high seas and so wintering waterbirds are mostly confined to the bays, probably moving according to the weather. Great Northern and Red-throated Divers are regular in Claggain Bay, in the extreme south-east, often with the occasional Black-throated. Great Northerns can also be seen in Port Ellen Bay, where up to 50 Goldeneye have been counted in the winter months, as well as in Saligo Bay in the north-west.

Sea cliffs

Islay has extensive sea cliffs, especially around the Oa and in places along the west coast of the Rinns, for example, south of Kilchiaran and at the northern end between Smaull and Saligo. Given the existence of these cliffs and the presence of relatively fertile seas around the island, the seabird colonies are disappointingly small, with most colonies consisting of no more than a few hundred pairs of Guillemots, Razorbills, Kittiwakes and Fulmars. The main reason for the small numbers would appear to be the lack of suitable ledges on which they can nest; the rock comprising the cliffs is not the right kind to produce such typical seabird nesting sites. This is borne out by the occurrence of a very large colony of seabirds on the west coast of nearby

Colonsay, where there are over 40,000 pairs of the four commonest species compared with fewer than 6,000 on Islay. Other species around Islay's coasts include over 200 pairs of Shags and several hundred pairs of Black Guillemot, the Oa being a particularly good area for them. The Oa also boasts two pairs of Golden Eagles and three or four pairs of Peregrines. There are six or seven pairs of the former on the island and perhaps a dozen pairs of the latter.

The hills

The highest cliff on Islay is below Beinn Mhor on the Oa, at just under 200 m. The highest hill is Beinn Bheigeir in the south-east of the island, rising to 456 m, over 300 m lower than the Paps of Jura, and made of the same hard and acidic rock, Jura quartzite, which forms most of the two hilly areas of Islay, in the east and in the north. For this reason, they are not particularly rich in birds, though a walk in the late spring and summer will be to the accompaniment of the fluting whistles of Golden Plover, several pairs of which breed. A few pairs of Ring Ouzel breed around Beinn Bheigeir. On the lower slopes of the hills, and especially where patches of heather flourish, a handful of pairs of Merlin and some further pairs of Hen Harriers breed, together with Curlews and the ubiquitous Meadow Pipit.

Farmland

The agriculture of Islay is almost entirely devoted to rearing sheep and cattle. Most of the farmland is therefore pasture which is ploughed and reseeded every few years to produce a fresh sward. In wetter areas, rushes quickly appear in the fields and may take over completely if the farmer decides the field cannot be better drained. On the higher ground, the grass is reseeded less frequently, if at all. Arable fields occupy only a small part of each farm and are mainly fodder crops such as kale, beet and barley.

It is not known when geese first started wintering on Islay, but the first major reference to them, in the 1890s, mentioned that the Barnacle Geese were causing agricultural damage. This has continued to the present day. The first good count of the geese was in the 1950s, when there were c.8,000 Barnacles and 2,500 Greenland Whitefronts. A long period of increase followed which, apart from some short-lived declines in the late 1970s, continued to the end of the 1990s. Since then, numbers appear to have levelled off at 35-40,000 Barnacle Geese and 8-10,000 Greenland Whitefronts.

This huge increase in numbers coincided with steadily improving farming practices, with larger fields, better grass mixes and more fertiliser. All these factors, together with mostly very light shooting, helped the geese by increasing their winter survival and boosting their breeding success. Because of the serious effect that the geese can have on farm profitability, a government-funded management scheme pays the farmers the equivalent of what they are losing and is combined with scaring on the most vulnerable fields, the new reseeds.

If agricultural damage is the downside of the geese, their presence in such spectacular numbers helps the island economy by attracting many birdwatchers to come and see them, as well as the other avian riches of the island. There is always the chance of seeing a small Canada Goose or a Snow Goose among the flocks of Barnacles and Whitefronts, visitors from North America.

One of Islay's special birds is the Chough. Over 60 pairs breed, or about 20% of the British population. As well as natural nesting sites in cliff caves, up to a third of the pairs nest in buildings, particularly on and around farms where they can find one of their favourite foods, the leatherjacket, in the pastures and seek out the larvae of dung flies and beetles in the cowpats. On the dune areas at Machir Bay and Ardnave, the cattle are left out all winter especially to provide the Choughs with a year-round food supply, and flocks of feeding birds, often up to 50 strong, are regular in both areas.

Two other important species are also dependent on Islay's farmland. Farm buildings provide nesting sites for Islay's population of of about 25 pairs of Barn Owls which find ample mice and voles in the rougher pastures. The taller vegetation in the corners of fields and alongside ditches attracts Corncrakes. This species nearly disappeared altogether from Islay in the mid-1990s, when only four calling birds were heard. However, thanks to careful management, such as delaying mowing until the birds have finished breeding in the pastures, both on the RSPB's reserves and by farmers and crofters across the island, the population increased in the next ten years to over 50, a real conservation success story.

Beside the River Sorn

Spring

12

Grey Heron *Ardea cinerea* - stalking along the foreshore

Three small colonies, at Sunderland, Loch Allan and Kildalton, with occasional pairs elsewhere, for example Foreland and Gruinart, probably make up an island population of about 20 pairs. The birds can often be seen fishing around the shores of Loch Indaal and Loch Gruinart, as well as on the Gruinart Flats and in the shallows in sheltered sea bays and the larger freshwater lochs, such as Loch Gorm.

13

Mute Swan *Cygnus olor* - a pair fly past, the male on the right

Between six and ten pairs breed on the island. They nest both on freshwater lochs, including Lochs Allan, Ballygrant, nan Cadhan, and sometimes Ardnave, and also on the beach or on small islets along the east and south coasts, for example at Lagavulin, Ardbeg and Proaig. There is a very small tidal range on Islay, making nesting close to the tideline reasonably safe. Flocks of up to 10–15 occur in Loch Indaal and in Port Ellen Bay.

Red-legged Partridge *Alectoris rufa* - revealing its red legs

With undeniable optimism, there have been persistent attempts over the years to establish the Red-legged Partridge as a game bird. Releases of young birds first took place in the 1950s, but the birds rarely survived more than a few years. Further attempts in the 1980s and 1990s gradually became more successful and there are now small, apparently self-sustaining, populations, for example on the Rinns and in the Laggan Valley.

14

Grey Partridge *Perdix perdix* - better camouflaged than the Redleg

As with the Red-legged Partridge, there have been many releases in an attempt to add it to the available sporting quarry. However, this species has proved more difficult to establish and, while small coveys may be seen in the autumn following release, numbers have usually been greatly reduced by the following spring or even, in several years, none have survived.

Black Grouse *Tetrao tetrix* - two males spar on their lek

This scarce resident has declined greatly in recent decades. In the 1960s, there were several leks of 10–20 males on the island. Some have since been lost to forestry planting while the general decline seen over most of Scotland has affected Islay, too. Small numbers, usually no more than five together, can still be seen in scrub woodland and around the edges of the plantations, and on some of the more overgrown heather moors.

**Linnet *Carduelis carduelis* - a male in
breeding plumage**

There are probably at least 200–300 pairs breeding in gorse and
other scrub spread widely across the island. During the winter, flocks
of 100–200 gather to feed on stubbles and other weedy arable fields,
often mixed with other finches.

**Twite *Carduelis flavirostris* - a winter-plumage
bird feeding by a snow patch**

Up to 100 pairs breed, mainly around the coasts, on cliff tops and
among dunes, though some nest on inland rocky outcrops. The
population is boosted in winter by migrants with flocks on arable
arable stubbles of from 200 to 500, occasionally more.

Yellowhammer *Emberiza citrinella* - a male sings from the top of a spruce tree
This is a widespread but local breeder and often quite difficult to find considering there maybe as many as 50–75 pairs. These are found not just where one might expect, around farmland where there are hedgerows and in scrub areas, but also in remote coastal gullies, for example along the north coast. During the autumn and winter, flocks of 10–20 can sometimes be found feeding on weedy arable fields.

18

Goldfinch *Carduelis carduelis* - feeding on spring buds

This species was unknown on the island before the 1950s and was not proved to breed until 1971. Since then, it has become widespread if nowhere common, and there are now at least 100 breeding pairs, with flocks in the autumn and winter regularly reaching 20–25, concentrating on thistles and other seeding plants. Their liking for fruit trees as nesting sites has brought them into many gardens.

Chough *Pyrrhocorax pyrrhocorax* - a pair, which will stay together for life

Between 60 and 80 pairs breed on Islay, many in cliff caves but with several pairs in buildings, especially derelict houses and in barns. They are found over most of the island, except in the south-east. The best areas to see them outside the breeding season are among the sand dunes at Kilchoman and Ardnave, where the presence of year-round cattle helps to provide good feeding opportunities for the flocks of 40 or more birds.

Long-tailed Tit *Aegithalos caudatus* - Islay's daintiest bird

There are probably up to 50 breeding pairs, nesting in thicker scrub on the edges of woodlands and in the larger more overgrown gardens. Outside the breeding season, feeding parties of 10–20 are often encountered in the broad-leaved woodlands and larger conifer plantations.

Coal Tit *Parus ater* - at a garden feeder

This is the commonest tit species on the island with somewhere between 200 and 400 pairs. It is found in all types of woodland, but the need for nesting holes means that the older woodlands, broad-leaved and conifer are the most favoured. In the autumn and winter, small flocks occur in the woodland, sometimes mixed with other tits.

Woodpigeon *Columba palumbus* - an adult poses on a fence post
There is evidence of a recent decline, probably associated with the felling around 2000–2001 of the large blocks of conifer plantations in the Glen. They are still found in the major woodlands at, for example, Ballygrant, Bridgend, Foreland and Kildalton, but the former flocks of 50–100 which used to be encountered in the winter seem to have disappeared. Presumably, numbers may build up again when the newer forestry matures.

Lesser Redpoll *Carduelis cabaret* **- a male in spring plumage**

This local woodland breeder was formerly confined to a few of the larger broad-leaved woodlands, but its population grew as the conifer plantations in the Glen matured during the 1980s and 1990s and it has now begun to colonise the younger plantations on the Rinns. There are probably at least 50 pairs, which in winter may be joined by small numbers of migrants to form feeding flocks of up to 30 or 40.

22

Common Crossbill *Loxia curvirostra* **- males drinking at a pool**

An irregular visitor with small numbers arriving in summer and autumn, in most but not all years. Occasionally, as in 1980, 1982 and again in 1989, birds which had stayed through the winter nested in the conifer plantations in the Glen. In the first two years it was only a single pair, but perhaps as many as six pairs did so in 1989, though they were not present the following year.

Rook *Corvus frugilegus* - an adult feeding on a pasture

There are about ten rookeries on the island, in small woods or isolated clumps of trees in Port Charlotte, at Gruinart, near Ballygrant and around Port Ellen. There were about 200 pairs in the 1980s, but numbers have grown to nearly 400. Flocks of several hundred, often mixed with Jackdaws, can be seen feeding on the pastures during the autumn and winter, seeking the leatherjackets which comprise a good part of their diet.

24

Black-throated Diver *Gavia arctica* **- in breeding plumage**
A possible breeding pair was reported about 30 years ago, but it is mostly known as a winter visitor, present from about October to March, with the majority occurring on Loch Indaal, where up to ten can be seen most winters. A few can sometimes be found around the coast, particularly at Claggain Bay. Every so often a full summer-plumaged bird may appear on a freshwater loch, but only the one instance of a pair together.

Cormorant *Phalacrocorax carbo* - an adult revealing its white flank patch

It is uncertain whether this is a breeding species. It is present year-round and birds in summer plumage are seen regularly, as are immature birds in autumn. Yet the last breeding record was more than 30 years ago. The main haunt is Loch Indaal, where up to 30 are regular with peaks of over 50. It also shows up around the coasts and, occasionally, on freshwater lochs.

Shag *Phalacrocorax aristotelis* - an adult with a juvenile not long out of the nest

A census in 2000 found 286 breeding pairs, mainly on the cliffs of The Oa and the Rinns. Outside the breeding season, the largest numbers are found on Loch Indaal, and scattered around the coasts.

26

Fulmar *Fulmarus glacialis* - in dispute

Nearly 2,000 pairs breed on the cliffs around the island. Most of them are on the Oa and on the west side of the Rinns. The colonies are all quite small (less than 100 pairs). Good places to see them are on the Rinns at Kilchiaran, where they breed on the low cliffs around the head of the small bay, and also at Kilchoman, where there are nests nearly a kilometre inland behind the old church. Birds can be seen offshore throughout the year.

Shelduck *Tadorna tadorna* - a pair, the male is on the left
About 30 pairs breed around the coasts, including in Lochs Gruinart and Indaal, and also in sandy bays along the south coast. Their nests are often in rabbit holes and may be hundreds of metres inland, so that the adult female has to lead her ducklings to the shore through such hazards as fences and tall vegetation. During the winter, there can be up to 300 in Loch Gruinart and 150 in Loch Indaal.

Gadwall *Anas strepera* - a male showing its white speculum

Small numbers, usually less than ten, winter on the flooded fields of the RSPB's Loch Gruinart reserve, and occasionally at the head of Loch Indaal. Pairs have stayed into the late spring in several years, but the only confirmed breeding took place in 1995 and 2003. Very occasionally, there have been influxes of autumn migrants, probably from Iceland, when over 20 can be present very briefly in October or November.

Shoveler *Anas clypeata* - two males leaving the water

The creation of the flooded marsh at the RSPB Loch Gruinart reserve led to a considerable increase in breeding numbers. Single pairs probably bred in 1957 and 1970, but breeding on the marsh quickly became regular and now up to 12 pairs nest annually. Numbers present during the rest of the year have also increased, with 40–50 present on the marsh in most months, peaking at over 90. They are rare elsewhere on the island.

Tufted Duck *Aythya fuligula* **- two pairs on the sea**

Breeding occurs on many of the larger lochs, such as Allan, Ballygrant, nan Cadhan, Finlaggan, Gorm, Kinnabus and Skerrols, as well as on lochs in the moorland such as Loch Laingedail and the pools on Duich Moss. There may be between 30 and 50 pairs in total. Wintering birds, with the addition of migrants, are found on most of the same waters plus, for example, Ardnave Loch. Numbers rarely exceed 30 on any one water.

Eider Duck *Somateria mollissima* - four males accompany a female

This resident duck breeds around the coasts and gathers in flocks in winter in the sealochs of Gruinart and Indaal as well as in sheltered bays around the coasts. No-one has counted them, but there are probably a few hundred pairs. Some nests are close to the sea, perhaps under debris at the top of a beach, but others can be half a kilometre inland, making the journey to the sea by the newly hatched young somewhat hazardous.

Common Scoter *Melanitta nigra* - a male flaps its wings
A few pairs breed on one of the lochs. They were first discovered in the 1950s and since then there have been as many as a dozen pairs, or up to 10% of the UK population, but more recently only one or two pairs; the reason for the decline is unknown. A flock of from 30 to 70 is found all year round on Loch Indaal, usually well out in the middle somewhere between Gartbreck (south of Bowmore) and Bruichladdich.

Dunlin *Calidris alpina* - coming into their summer plumage

Small numbers breed around bog pools and on the wetter moorland with perhaps 50–100 pairs in all. Several hundred birds winter in Lochs Gruinart and Indaal and there is a small spring passage in March to April. Much larger numbers occur during the autumn migration, particularly in Loch Gruinart, where up to 3,000 have been recorded in July and August, concentrated on the sandflats at the head of the loch.

34

Ruff *Philomachus pugnax* - a male about to adopt its breeding finery
This species has become much more regular in the years since the marshland was created on the RSPB's Loch Gruinart reserve. Once very rare, they are now seen there nearly every spring, when mainly single birds appear, and again in autumn, when small flocks of 5–10, once a flock of over 40, are seen between July and November. Single birds may also occur around the head of Loch Indaal, and occasionally elsewhere.

Black-tailed Godwit *Limosa limosa* - in its breeding plumage

Like the Ruff, this species has become much more regular on the island since the marshland was created on the RSPB's Loch Gruinart reserve in 1992. Flocks of 10–20, occasionally up to 50, turn up at Gruinart every April and May, with further flocks, again up to 50, at the head of Loch Indaal and on the marshy ground beside Ardnave Loch. There is a smaller return passage between July and September.

Lesser Black-backed Gull *Larus fuscus* - an adult scavenging on the shore
Up to 300 pairs breed in small colonies which are scattered along the coast, for instance on the west side of the Rinns, as well as in a very few places inland, where they are usually in mixed colonies with Herring Gulls. This is a migrant species on Islay, the birds arriving in late February and March and departing again in September and October. Only a handful of birds are usually present in the winter months.

Arctic Skua *Stercorarius parasiticus* - a pale phase adult circles overhead

The few pairs which breed on Jura (just six in 2000) are the most southerly in Britain. They include both pale and dark phase birds. It is presumably these birds and perhaps visitors from colonies further north that are often seen in the Sound of Islay in the summer months. Small numbers regularly pass Frenchman's Rocks in spring and autumn.

Great Skua *Stercorarius skua* - a passing adult with its prominent wing flashes

The nearest breeding birds are in the Outer Hebrides, but passage migrants are seen almost every spring and autumn, less often in the summer. They are usually off the west coast but are occasionally spotted flying over Loch Indaal or Loch Gruinart.

Osprey *Pandion haliaetus* - plunging towards its prey

As the Scottish population has increased, so sightings on Islay have become more common and at least one, sometimes two, individuals are seen every year, most usually in the spring and autumn. With several pairs now breeding in mainland Argyll, perhaps a pair will find Islay attractive before too long. Certainly, the visiting birds often fish in the trout lochs on the island, while Loch Gruinart is another favoured feeding site.

Golden Eagle *Aquila chrysaetos* - an adult surveys its territory from a tree top

There are up to seven resident pairs, nesting on coastal cliffs and inland crags. Once heavily persecuted, the species is now probably back to its optimum number on the island. There are at least two former ranges which are not now occupied, but they can probably no longer provide an adequate food supply to support a breeding pair. Young birds wander widely throughout the year and can be seen anywhere on the island.

Pied Wagtail *Motacilla alba yarrellii* - a male in winter plumage

A widespread and common breeder found along the shore, in the dunes, around farmsteads, and, in autumn and winter, feeding in flocks along the roadsides. There may be up to 300 pairs in total. Autumn and winter flocks often total 20–30 birds.

White Wagtail *Motacilla alba alba* - a female feeding in shallow water

This is the mainland European form of the Pied Wagtail. It occurs here on passage in April and May and, less commonly, during August to October. Often there are just scattered single birds, but flocks of up to 20 or more sometimes turn up, especially in spring.

Wheatear *Oenanthe oenanthe* - a male flicks its wings in display

Wheatears are commonest in areas of short vegetation, e.g. coastal dunes, grassland and uplands, and particularly where there are stone dykes in which to nest. There are probably at least 500 breeding pairs, perhaps more. The first arrivals are from mid-March and occasional birds stay into early November. Slightly larger and brighter birds belonging to the Greenland race *O. o. leucorrhoa* are sometimes seen in spring and autumn.

Chiffchaff *Phylloscopus collybita* - hunting for food among reeds

Only relatively few pairs breed, probably no more than 20, mainly in the larger woodlands and especially those with good scrubby understorey. They arrive early, before the end of March, sing actively for a couple of months and then fall silent and become very inconspicuous. Occasional birds are reported during the winter, some at which are very grey in plumage and so probably migrants from a different subspecies, either *P. c. abietinus* or *tristis*.

Common Whitethroat *Sylvia communis* - a male sings from its perch
A widespread breeder of woodland edges and scrub, including in clearings and along the rides of the conifer plantations. The present island population, estimated at 150–200 pairs, was probably somewhat larger 40 years ago before numbers across Europe declined sharply following severe drought in the African wintering grounds. The first arrivals take place in the second half of April, with the last birds noted in October.

44

House Martin *Delichon urbica* - gathering mud for its nest

There is evidence of an increase in the breeding population in recent years, as householders frequently report first time nesting. Some quite large colonies exist, of up to 20 or 25 nests, but also many ones and twos scattered through the villages or on isolated houses. Cliff nesting has occasionally been reported. There are certainly 200–300 pairs on the island, perhaps more. The birds arrive in mid-April and depart in October.

Wren *Troglodytes troglodytes* - momentarily still
There are few parts of the island, other than the higher hills, which are without Wrens. They can be heard belting out their song in a great variety of habitats, whether in woodland, scrub and gardens or along stone dykes crossing moorland or among the rocks at the foot of sea cliffs. The island population certainly numbers several hundred pairs.

Dunnock *Prunella modularis* - on a bramble stem
A resident species that occurs in all kinds of wooded and shrubby areas, including gardens where it is frequent at bird tables. It regularly colonises new plantations, staying in the rides and clearings after the trees have grown up. A difficult bird to census, but there may be around 200–300 pairs breeding on the island.

Reed Bunting *Emberiza schoeniclus* - a male on a budding ash twig

A widespread breeder found in most damp, well vegetated areas, especially overgrown ditches, reedbeds, in bushes by lochs and in scrub close to water. Some pairs seem to tolerate drier conditions around farmland and moorland edges. The best estimate of breeding pairs is about 200 pairs. Some flocks occur in the autumn and winter often mixed with finches. These sometimes number up to 50.

Jackdaw *Corvus monedula* - a pair on the roof of their nesting building

Several hundred pairs breed in holes of all kinds, often in trees, but probably most are in derelict buildings and around farms, as well as in cliff caves and, occasionally, holes in tall sand dunes. Outside the breeding season, they gather in flocks of hundreds and feed on the farmland, often mixed with Rooks. These flocks mostly roost at night in trees, occasionally in buildings, with one record of a flock roosting on the beach of the Big Strand.

Carrion Crow *Corvus corone* **- bathing vigorously**

A few birds, from one to five, are seen most years and in most months, sometimes with Hooded Crows, at other times solitary. Occasional pairs have been recorded, but they are not known to have bred, though a mixed pair with a Hooded Crow did nest some years ago.

48

Hooded Crow *Corvus cornix* **- dealing with a winkle on the shore**

Although subject to some control by keepers, this is a widespread and numerous bird, breeding in woodland, inland gullies and around the coasts. There may be around 200–300 pairs, while flocks of up to 30 or 40 are quite common at all seasons.

Looking across Loch Indaal to the eastern hills

Summer

Red-throated Diver *Gavia stellata* - a breeding bird with its chicks

Less than ten pairs breed each summer, choosing a wide variety of nesting locations, from the banks of small lochans to islets in large lochs, and mainly in the hills, but with at least one lowland site. The nesting lochs are very traditional; one has been used regularly since the early 1970s. Outside the breeding season, up to 30–40 birds are present on Loch Indaal, mainly in the inner part, with smaller numbers around the coasts.

Little Grebe *Tachybaptus ruficollis* - a breeding bird with its chick

The trilling calls can be heard in spring on several of the more fertile lowland freshwater lochs, including Ballygrant, nan Cadhan, Finlaggan, Lossit and Tallant. The birds are quite territorial and it is rare to have more than one pair per loch. The stripey youngsters appear in June or July and then disperse once fledged. In the winter, birds may appear on other lochs, e.g. Ardnave and Skerrols, as well as on Lochs Gruinart and Indaal.

Gannet *Sula bassana* - an adult glides overhead

Birds from the huge colony of some 40,000 pairs on Ailsa Craig in the Clyde can been seen between May and October making their spectacular fishing dives off the coasts, and even right into the inner part of Loch Indaal. During the same period, lines of birds will be passing the west coast of the Rinns making their long journeys between colony and feeding grounds. Dark-plumaged young birds turn up in the autumn.

Greylag Goose *Anser anser* - a family party

Although the first breeding record was as recently as 1997, pairs can now be found quite widely, especially around Loch Gorm and on some of the offshore islets, such as Nave and Texa. Many hundreds used to winter in the 1950s, but these disappeared in the 1970s. More recently, 100–150 are present all winter, perhaps mainly local breeders, but ringed birds from the Iceland-breeding population have also been seen.

Common Gull *Larus canus* - a pair bathing in a freshwater lochan

A few hundred pairs breed in many small colonies, which can be inland as well as close to the coast. There appears to have been a decline in recent years, part of a wider decline in western Scotland, the reasons for which are uncertain. Flocks of many hundreds, occasionally a thousand or more, can be found in Loch Gruinart and Loch Indaal all the year round, though with the largest numbers in the autumn and winter.

Kittiwake *Rissa tridactyla* - on their nests with well-grown chicks

Breeding mainly on the west coast of the Rinns and on the Oa, a total of 775 pairs was found during a full survey in 2000. This represents a 20% decline from the 975 pairs found in 1986. Birds are seen at sea or passing Frenchman's Rocks in all months of the year, but especially between August and November, while they are scarcest in the middle of the winter.

Common Tern *Sterna hirundo* **- a pair displaying**

This is an uncommon breeding bird, with a handful of pairs found at just a few sites, some of which are used for a few years and then abandoned for a time before coming back into use again. Among them are the skerries at Blackrock and Gartnatra in Loch Indaal, the Big Strand, islets in Loch Gorm and on some of the skerries off the south-east coast of the island. A survey in 1986 found 23 pairs, but there were only 10 pairs in 2000.

Arctic Tern *Sterna paradisea* - an adult flies past

This is the commonest tern breeding on the island, with between 200 and 300 pairs. Small colonies, of rarely more than 50 pairs, breed on islets and beaches in Lochs Gruinart and Indaal, on headlands and islands around the Rinns, in the Sound of Islay and round the south-east coast. As is usual for this species, both colony size and position varies between years and a flourishing colony one year may be completely deserted the next.

Little Tern *Sterna albifrons* - feeding its incubating mate

About 10–15 pairs breed regularly at one location on the island while one or two pairs breed in most but not all years at three or four other sites to give a fairly consistent total of around 20 pairs on the island over the last 20–25 years. Whether regular or erratic, nearly all the breeding attempts each year take place within colonies of the larger, more aggressive, Arctic Tern, giving the Little Tern much needed protection from predators.

Guillemot *Uria aalge* - on a breeding ledge, with two Razorbills

Small colonies are scattered round the Oa and along the west coast of the Rinns to a total of nearly 1,500 pairs in the last full survey, in 2000. This is only about half the number counted 15 years before but there is no obvious reason for the decline as most other seabirds, including the Razorbill, have increased over the same period.

Razorbill *Alca torda* - on the look out

Breeds, usually with Guillemots, in the same scattered small colonies on the Oa and the west coast of the Rinns. The total of about 1,750 pairs counted in 2000 was up from just under 1,500 in the mid-1980s. Both Razorbills and Guillemots pass Frenchman's Rocks in their thousands daily, especially in autumn and winter, presumably on feeding movements associated with the offshore tidal currents. They are also numerous on the ferry crossings.

60

Black Guillemot *Cepphus grylle* **- a pair in summer plumage**
There is a concentration of several hundred birds around the cliff-girt coast of the Oa, while scattered breeding pairs occur almost everywhere around the island except the sandy stretches. As well as natural nesting holes in cliffs and among boulders, pairs also breed in man-made structures, such as under piers and even in ruined buildings on the shore. The birds are resident, adopting their mostly white winter plumage in the autumn.

Ringed Plover *Charadrius hiaticula* - guarding its chicks

Just about every shingle and sandy beach round the island has breeding pairs, often several in a short stretch, nesting just above high-water mark, though occasionally a short distance inland. A one-kilometre stretch of shore of Loch Indaal a few years ago held no less than 16 pairs, and the island total is certainly several hundred. Flocks in Lochs Gruinart and Indaal reach up to 500 during spring and autumn passage.

Lapwing *Vanellus vanellus* - with a well-grown youngster

A significant concentration of over 200 pairs breed on the Gruinart Flats, within the RSPB's reserve, where the low-lying fields are managed for them by providing plenty of shallow standing water full of invertebrate food. Breeding also occurs in older, wetter pastures elsewhere, but not on the more intensively farmed fields. Some stay the winter, but the majority depart in October, returning again from about the middle of February.

Common Snipe *Gallinago gallinago* - on a fencepost, a surprisingly frequent sight
The familiar drumming can be heard in spring over many of the wetter areas of the island, but perhaps especially on the Rinns, where up to 60 pairs breed on the RSPB's Loch Gruinart reserve, benefiting, like the Lapwing, from the wetland management carried out there. The total island population is probably at least 200–300 pairs. Occasional autumn and winter flocks of up to 50 birds suggest the presence of migrants.

Curlew *Numenius arquata* - and chick

Breeding pairs can be found spread widely across the island on the moorland and rougher pastures. There were nearly 150 pairs on the Rinns in 1994, so the island population is probably at least double that, possibly more. Outside the breeding season, the largest flocks occur in Lochs Gruinart and Indaal, with around 500 wintering in each. Smaller flocks are frequently seen feeding in the damper pastures elsewhere on the island.

Redshank *Tringa totanus* - showing its prominent red 'shanks'

The presence of over 100 breeding pairs makes the RSPB's Loch Gruinart reserve an important site for this species. Many of the small marshy areas where it formerly bred have been lost to more intensive cultivation and drainage. It nevertheless remains a widespread breeder across the island totalling perhaps 300–400 pairs. Winter flocks occur in Lochs Gruinart and Indaal with autumn passage in August at the former site.

Water Rail *Rallus aquaticus* - it is rarely seen out in the open

The status of this secretive bird is poorly known. Reports of its squealing courtship calls suggest that up to four pairs may occur in the wet ditches and reed areas around the head of Loch Gruinart, where young have been seen. Birds have also been heard in the reedbeds at Braigo and Foreland, and at Lochs Ballygrant, Fada, Gorm and Tallant, but it is not known at which, if any, of these it breeds regularly. Reports in winter, when birds may feed out in the open, are more widespread.

Spotted Crake *Porzana porzana* - an equally rare view out in the open

An almost annual visitor that announces its presence with its far-carrying 'whiplash' call. Prior to 1989, there were just two records, in 1896 and 1973. Since then, however, the species has turned up nearly every year, always in the Gruinart–Gorm area. In most years, just a single calling bird is heard, but occasionally two or even three turn up. The sighting of a young bird at Gruinart in 1993 strongly suggests that breeding has occurred.

Common Sandpiper *Actitis hypoleucos* - uttering its loud whistling call

Any rocky or stony shore will satisfy this migrant wader as a breeding territory. These can be along stretches of shingle beach or among low rocks, a length of burn or river, or on the seemingly barren shore of a remote hill loch where few other birds occur. They arrive in the first half of April and soon make their presence noticed with their whistling calls and jerky flight low over the water. They have normally departed by the end of

Herring Gull *Larus argentatus* - on its nest among the thrift

Up to 500 pairs breed in several small coastal colonies, particularly on the Rinns and around the Oa, as well as on Texa and Nave islands. There are a few inland colonies, where they are usually mixed with Lesser Black-backed Gulls. They are widespread and common throughout the year and there is a regular concentration of them at the refuse disposal tip south of Bowmore.

Corncrake *Crex crex* - an unusual view of one calling out in the open

Once a common and widespread species, annual censuses since 1991 revealed a marked decline almost to the point of extinction, with only four birds heard in 1998. Fortunately, active management by the RSPB on its reserves, together with farmers and crofters adopting Corncrake-friendly farming techniques, especially by delaying grass mowing, has produced a remarkable recovery, with 10 in 2003, 30 in 2004 and over 50 in 2005.

Skylark *Alauda arvensis* - approaching its nest with food for its young

This is one of the commoner breeding species on the island, with an estimated 5,000–8,000 breeding pairs. A survey of much of the Rinns in 1994 found no less than 2,000 pairs, with particularly high densities on the moorland with its abundance of invertebrate food and plentiful nest sites among the heather and other taller vegetation. During the autumn and winter, flocks of from 100 to 300 are frequent on farmland.

Cuckoo *Cuculus canorus* - a male takes to the wing

Cuckoos arrive on Islay from about the middle of April, though some years not until early May. They are widespread across the island, particularly on moorland adjacent to woodland or scrub, though not particularly common, indeed anecdotal evidence suggests they are less numerous than they used to be. The main host species for their eggs is the Meadow Pipit, which is one of the island's most abundant small birds.

Marsh Harrier *Circus aeruginosus* - an adult female in flight

This is now a more or less annual visitor having been no more than a rare vagrant in the 1970s. Single birds appear mainly in the spring, sometimes being seen for only a few days, but occasionally staying right through the summer.. The increase in sightings parallels a substantial increase in the British breeding population in the last 30 years, with breeding now occurring at localities in Scotland.

72

Red Kite *Milvus milvus* - an adult soars overhead hunting

Once a rare vagrant, it appeared regularly on Islay in the early 1990s as birds from the re-introduction programme in the north of Scotland began wandering south and west for the winter. Some individuals stayed for several months, others passed through and were also seen returning in spring. When breeding commenced close to their release area in the mid-1990s, records on Islay declined as the young birds no longer disperse this far.

Hen Harrier *Circus cyaneus* - an adult male scanning the ground for prey
Formerly breeding in the 19th century, they were exterminated because of the perceived conflict with sporting interests, especially grouse shooting. This no longer takes place on the island and, since the late 1960s, the species has been able to re-establish itself. The forestry planting in the 1980s provided ideal nesting and feeding habitat and led to a considerable increase in numbers which has since been largely maintained.

Sparrowhawk *Accipiter nisus* - an adult male with prey
The commonest small bird of prey, breeding in virtually all the major woodlands on the island, as well as in many smaller copses and in extensive areas of scrub. Numbers have probably increased in recent years, perhaps given a boost by the maturing of the forestry plantations, and a population of 40 or more pairs seems realistic. They hunt widely in winter and are common visitors to larger gardens.

Kestrel *Falco tinnunculus* - an adult female at rest

No more than ten pairs breed, fewer than the island might be thought able to support. They nest on inland and coastal crags and, sometimes, in ruined buildings, hunting over farmland, moorland and the forestry plantations, indeed anywhere that might support their principal food of mice and voles. There may be a small autumn movement to the island as numbers in winter appear slightly higher than at other times of year.

Peregrine *Falco peregrinus* - an adult male perches close to its nesting ledge
About 15 pairs breed but, in common with other parts of western Scotland, numbers have fallen slightly over the last 20 years. Most nest sites are on traditional cliffs around the coasts, but a few pairs nest on inland crags and the sides of steep gullies. The birds range all over the island during the winter and can be seen almost anywhere, though perhaps most regularly around Lochs Gruinart and Indaal hunting ducks, waders and gulls.

Dotterel *Charadrius morinellus* - an adult male in breeding habitat

This is a scarce, but nearly annual, migrant with small numbers, usually between one and ten, seen on spring passage in April or May and in August or September. The birds can turn up almost anywhere on the island, often in well-watched places like Loch Gruinart, but also on farmland well away from the coast. In 1990, a pair was seen on the summit ridge of Beinn Bheigeir in early June and may have bred there.

Sand Martin *Riparia riparia* - feeding its hungry youngsters

There are several small colonies, mostly of 10–20 pairs, scattered along the River Laggan from the High Road to its mouth, as well as in sand dunes behind the Big Strand and at Ardnave, and in a burnside bank at Kilchiaran. Feeding birds can be seen hunting for insects over lochs and pools. This is one of the earliest spring migrants, arriving from the middle of March. The last ones are generally seen in late September or October.

Swallow *Hirundo rustica* - an adult on a typical perch

There are few farms or derelict buildings on the island without breeding Swallows, and they also find their way into quite small garages and garden sheds and build their nests inside. There must be several hundred pairs on the island. The first arrivals appear in early April and it is quite usual to see late stayers at the end of October or even early November. Before they depart, flocks of 50–100 are a regular sight on overhead wires.

Ring Ouzel *Turdus torquatus* - a male with its prominent white crescent

This species was first proved to breed in the eastern hills as recently as 1991. In the next few years, there were thought to be up to five pairs, but the area has rarely been checked since and the true status and current extent of the breeding population is uncertain. Occasional birds are seen on spring and autumn passage.

Redstart *Phoenicurus phoenicurus* - a male in breeding plumage

This is another species of uncertain status. In the 1970s and 1980s, a few pairs undoubtedly bred every year in the older woodlands, for example at Ardnahoe, Ballygrant and Kildalton. However, the last report of a singing male was as long ago as 1989 and no birds have been seen in these former breeding sites for several recent years, despite searching and despite the occurrence of one or two spring migrants in late April and early May in some years.

Song Thrush *Turdus philomelos* - in full song

The island probably holds a breeding population of several hundred pairs. Although the species has declined in some parts of Britain, here it still seems to be doing well, whether in woodlands, scrub or gardens. Some autumn passage occurs most years, with flocks up to 25 to be seen in October, but few of these appear to winter, and at least some of the local breeding birds move south at this time, too.

82

Whinchat *Saxicola rubetra* - a male perched on a dead bramble
This migrant arrives in the second half of April and into early May, and breeds widely in moorland and scrub areas. The forestry plantations on the Rinns held good numbers when the trees were young. It seems likely that there are between 100 and 200 pairs with little sign of any change in overall numbers in the last 20–30 years, though the forestry may have given the population a temporary boost.

Stonechat *Saxicola torquata* - a male taking a caterpillar to its nest
This close relative of the Whinchat is at least as widespread and probably commoner overall, with perhaps 250 or more breeding pairs. It is equally found on areas of rough moorland and scrub edges, being particularly fond of gorse and large bramble patches. Although often regarded as a resident in western Scotland there is evidence from reduced numbers in winter of at least some autumn emigration by our breeding birds.

Tree Pipit *Anthus trivialis* - gathering food for its chicks

A few pairs breed around the edges of the larger broad-leaved woodlands, for example at Ballygrant, Bridgend and Kildalton. Singing males have also been heard beside the patches of oak woodland in the south-east of the island near Claggain Bay. There are reports which suggest that there may have been up to 20 pairs in the 1970s and 1980s, but there seem to be fewer than that now, perhaps less than 10 pairs.

Grasshopper Warbler *Locustella naevia* **- singing from its perch in a hawthorn**

The thin, high reeling song is heard in May and early June coming from damp, overgrown habitats, such as reedy swamps, scrub, hedges alongside ditches and in and around the edges of young plantations. The population seems to have increased in the last 20 or so years and the island now supports perhaps up to 100 pairs. The earliest reported arrival was in late April and the birds have mostly departed by mid-August..

Sedge Warbler *Acrocephalus schoenobaenus* - in typical scrub willow habitat
Another distinctive songster which rattles away in reedbeds, scrub, young plantations, overgrown ditches and other damp areas. It is common and widespread across the island and there could be as many as 750 or more pairs, based on a survey of part of the Rinns which found nearly 200 singing males in 1994. They are occasionally heard by mid-April, but more usually a little later, and are last seen in September.

Wood Warbler *Phylloscopus sibilatrix* - at its nest on the ground

Small numbers, perhaps 10–20 pairs, breed in the older broad-leaved woodlands, with most records coming from the woods around Ballygrant, Bridgend and Kildalton. They arrive at the very end of April, while there are few sightings after July or early August.

Goldcrest *Regulus regulus* - exploring a conifer

Although always quite common in the larger broad-leaved woodlands, the maturing of the conifer plantations in the Glen certainly increased the population through the 1980s and 1990s, though it may now have declined a little since the trees were largely felled a few years ago. There are a possible 150–250 pairs which may increase again as other plantations develop. A few migrants arrive in autumn, with some spring passage, too.

Blackcap *Sylvia atricapilla* **- a male feeding on ivy berries**

Small numbers of singing males are present in the broad-leaved woodlands, especially at Bridgend, every summer and breeding probably occurs most years, though rarely proved. It is quite frequent as an autumn migrant and there are several records of single wintering birds, including coming to bird tables.

Garden Warbler *Sylvia borin* **- on a bramble**

One or two are occasionally heard singing in spring in the broad-leaved woodlands at Ballygrant and Bridgend, but this happened more in the 1980s and early 1990s than recently. Breeding has never been proved, but it may well have occurred.

Willow Warbler *Phylloscopus trochilus* - in full song

This may well be the island's commonest breeding warbler, with possibly as many as 1,000 pairs. They breed not only in all the larger woodlands of all types, but also in windbreaks, small patches of scrub, young plantations and even quite small gardens, provided there are trees. They are among the earliest migrants to arrive, at the very end of March and early April, with the main departure in September.

Bullfinch *Pyrrhula pyrrhula* - a male in its stunning plumage
The most likely place to encounter a pair of these birds is in the larger broad-leaved woodlands and also in more mature conifer plantations. Despite the vivid colouring of the male, they can be quite secretive and it is difficult to know the size of the population, but 30 or more pairs seems likely. In the winter months, pairs and family parties range more widely and may visit larger gardens.

Spotted Flycatcher *Muscicapa striata* - in characteristic pose

Although most Spotted Flycatchers probably breed in the older broad-leaved woodland, pairs regularly nest in larger gardens, using nestboxes or ledges in old walls. First arrivals are not until the middle of May by which time, because the trees are already coming into leaf, they can be difficult to spot and so the island population has to be put at a tentative 30 or so pairs.

**Tawny Owl *Strix aluco* - roosting during the day
in a tree**

About ten pairs live in the broad-leaved woodland, both large and small, including Foreland, Gruinart, Bridgend, Tallant, Ballygrant, Kildalton and Kilnaughton. The sites are very traditional; one has been used for well over 20 years.

**Short-eared Owl *Asio flammeus* - perched but
looking for prey**

Variable numbers of pairs nest depending on vole densities in the plantations, i.e. numbers ranged between 0 and 20+ pairs on the Rinns during the 1990s. They favour plantations and open areas of heather moorland and rough vegetation.

Rowans beside the High Road

Autumn

Red Grouse *Lagopus lagopus* - three young birds among the heather
In the 1920s and 1930s, very large bags were shot on the island but, by the 1950s, the population had already begun the steep decline which has continued to this day as it has across so much of western Scotland. Only very small numbers now breed on both lowland and hill moorland and it seems probable that there are no more than 50 pairs on the island with little chance of a return to the numbers of former times.

Great Crested Grebe *Podiceps cristatus* - an adult still showing traces of breeding plumage
Back in 1979, a pair bred on Ardnave Loch, but it was a one-off event as the pair never returned and there has been no attempt since. It is now an irregular autumn and winter visitor, usually singly, occasionally two together, and nearly always seen on salt water, for example in Loch Indaal or in a sheltered bay round the coast. The only recent occurrences on fresh water have been on Loch Gorm.

Whooper Swan *Cygnus cygnus* - a flock, all adults, taking off

Several hundred birds, coming from Iceland, pass through every October and November. The flocks, which may number up to 100, sometimes stay a few hours, sometimes for several weeks, feeding on the stubble fields around Loch Gorm and Loch Gruinart. Other birds feed on the *Zostera* beds in Loch Indaal, just east of Bowmore. The numbers gradually dwindle through November and only a handful of birds usually spend the winter.

Pink-footed Goose *Anser brachyrhynchus* **- on the alert**

This species winters in very small numbers, usually among the flocks of Barnacles and Whitefronts. They are most often single birds, pairs or small flocks rarely totalling more than ten. In addition, every September and October, a few flocks of 100 or more are seen on migration from Iceland, often landing on the sandflats of Loch Gruinart, or occasionally on the adjacent fields, and resting for a while before setting off again.

Light-bellied Brent Goose *Branta bernicla hrota* - a small flock feeding on the shore

Islay lies on the migration route of these geese from arctic Canada to Ireland and, every autumn and spring, flocks sometimes hundreds strong are seen passing overhead or landing in Loch Gruinart or Loch Indaal before moving on. Small numbers, usually no more than 20, often stay through the winter around the shores of Loch Indaal, and occasional ones and twos can be found in the flocks of Barnacles.

Teal *Anas crecca* - a wheeling flock

About 50 pairs or perhaps more breed around lochs and beside small pools in boggy moorland areas. Migrants from Iceland begin arriving in September and stay through until March. Up to 3,000 are present on the RSPB's Loch Gruinart reserve, the shallow water, rich in seeds and invertebrates, making ideal wintering habitat. A further 300 winter at the head of Loch Indaal as well as smaller flocks on some freshwater lochs.

Pochard *Aythya ferina* - a male wing-flapping
A wintering duck, appearing on many of the more fertile freshwater lochs, e.g. Ardnave, Ballygrant and Skerrols, as well as on Loch Gorm and, very rarely, on Loch Indaal, from about September onwards and staying to March and April, occasionally into May. Numbers are mostly small, less than 20–30, but larger flocks sometimes appear, for example up to 200 on Loch Skerrols in winter 1996–7.

Common Buzzard *Buteo buteo* - searching the ground for invertebrates

This is the commonest bird of prey on Islay with at least 50 breeding pairs nesting in woodlands, isolated trees and on ledges of inland crags and gorges. They can frequently be seen perching on telegraph poles and fence posts along the roadside. The species was once much scarcer than it is now because of persecution but, when this ceased, the species quickly occupied all the parts of the island from which it was formerly excluded.

White-tailed Eagle *Haliaeetus albicilla* - an adult hunting low over the sea
Old records and Gaelic placenames suggest that several pairs bred in the 19th century. As elsewhere in Scotland, they became extinct but, since the re-introduction programme started on Rum in the 1970s, with more than 30 pairs now breeding in the Hebrides, including on Mull, sightings of birds, mainly immatures, are becoming regular here. It is perhaps only a matter of time before the species breeds on the island once more.

Merlin *Falco columbarius* - a male perched on a mossy boulder

There are less than ten pairs breeding on the island. They tend to occupy the same territory over many years, nearly always in a remote valley with banks of deep heather in which they conceal their nests. In October, migrants arrive from Iceland, staying through the winter before departing in April. These birds often prey on the large finch flocks which gather to feed on seeds among harvested crops such as barley stubbles and turnips.

Golden Plover *Pluvialis apricaria* - roosting, with a Lapwing, at the tide edge

A walk in the hills in early summer will be accompanied by the fluting whistles of nesting Golden Plover. Some tens of pairs breed on the higher ground in both the north and east of the island. Flocks of several hundred birds have long been regular on passage in autumn and spring but, in recent years, up to 1,500 are now wintering, roosting on the sands at the head of Loch Indaal and flying out to feed in the surrounding farmland.

Oystercatcher *Haematopus ostralegus* - an adult in winter plumage

At least 200–300 pairs breed, the majority of them around the coast, particularly at the top of shingle beaches or on coastal grassland within a few hundred metres of the sea. A few pairs can also be found nesting well inland, for example along the Laggan River or beside Loch Gorm. Flocks of several hundred birds are present in both Lochs Gruinart and Indaal throughout the year, peaking in winter at up to 500 and 750, respectively.

Knot *Calidris canutus* - an adult moulting out of its summer plumage

Knot occur mainly on spring and autumn passage, but can be seen throughout the year, as birds occasionally spend the winter or stay into the summer. Small flocks appear in February and build to a peak in April when there may be over 100 in both Loch Gruinart and Loch Indaal. The larger autumn passage begins in August and continues to October or November, with peaks of up to 150 in Loch Gruinart and 300 in Loch Indaal.

Sanderling *Calidris alba* - scurrying along the beach

The largest flocks are seen on spring and autumn passage, but small numbers can turn up in any month of the year and on any of the island's beaches and sandflats. The main spring passage takes place between February and May when flocks of 20 or 30 occur around the island. The autumn passage involves similar numbers of birds seen between August and November, but larger flocks, of up to 100, are sometimes reported.

Woodcock *Scolopax rusticola* - resting unusually out in the open

This has to be one of Islay's least known birds. It probably breeds in most of the larger, damper woodlands, with roding seen or heard in the spring at, for example, Bridgend, Kildalton and Kilnaughton, but there has been no estimate of the numbers of breeding birds. Autumn passage and winter visitors can be quite numerous, particularly when cold weather occurs on the mainland.

Curlew Sandpiper *Calidris ferruginea* - an adult still showing some summer plumage colour

Single birds, occasionally small flocks of 10–20 birds, turn up in most autumns, but only very rarely in spring. The majority of sightings are in Lochs Gruinart and Indaal.

Little Stint *Calidris minuta* - a juvenile feeding on the mudflats

A scarce, but almost annual, autumn passage migrant, with small parties of birds, rarely more than five together and often just singles, though with a maximum of 18, turning up in most years between July and November, though usually in August and September. The most frequent locations are Lochs Gruinart and Indaal. There is just one spring record.

Wood Sandpiper *Tringa glareola* - an adult wading through the marsh

A passage migrant that is becoming more regular. This may be because not only are the conditions of the marsh on the RSPB's Loch Gruinart reserve much to this species liking, but the presence of the hide means there is a good chance that they will be seen. Certainly, from being only rarely recorded, it is now almost annual.

110

Green Sandpiper *Tringa ochropus* - an adult feeding in a burn

This is another species, like the Wood Sandpiper, whose apparent increase in recent years may be due to better conditions at Loch Gruinart both for the bird and for seeing it. Most records are of one to three birds, only rarely in spring, more usually in July to September.

111

Bar-tailed Godwit *Limosa lapponica* - in winter plumage

Flocks of up to 100–200 are present throughout the year in both Lochs Gruinart and Indaal. In the former loch, they feed widely at low tide, finding a rocky skerry or spit to roost on when the tide is in. The birds in Loch Indaal show a similar behaviour, but roost and feed in the inner part of the loch, especially along the shore west of Bowmore and round to Blackrock. It is rare to see them anywhere else on the island.

Whimbrel *Numenius phaeopus* - an adult in flight over the sea
A spring and autumn passage migrant with flocks, usually of 20–50, but occasionally up to 100, occurring in April and May and again from July to September. The occasional bird has summered. Most of the flocks feed on pastures near the coast, with several traditional sites on the east side of the Rinns and round Loch Gorm. They also feed on the sandflats of Lochs Gruinart and Indaal.

Black-headed Gull *Larus ridibundus* - an adult in winter plumage

A few hundred pairs breed in widely scattered small colonies, both coastal and inland. They are found over much of the island throughout the year but are scarcer in winter. The largest wintering flocks are at Loch Gruinart and Loch Indaal, with between 100 and 150 regular at both. These are only about half the totals that were present about 15 years ago, but whether breeding numbers have similarly declined is not known.

Sandwich Tern *Sterna sandvicensis* - an adult in winter plumage

Small numbers, usually under five, are seen most years, either in the spring or in late summer and autumn. A number of times an adult has been seen with a juvenile in August suggesting breeding has occurred not all that far away. The nearest known breeders are about 80 kilometres away in Donegal, Eire.

114

Puffin *Fratercula arctica* - coming into a splash landing

This was reported to be an abundant breeder in the 19th century, especially on the Oa, but severe declines took place and it had become very scarce by 1950s. A very few pairs may still breed as birds are occasionally seen carrying fish near the west coast seabird colonies at Sanaig and Lossit, though none were seen during a boat survey round the island in 2000. Small numbers are quite frequently seen offshore and from the ferry.

Kingfisher *Alcedo atthis* - a female looking for a fish

Single birds appear occasionally, mainly in autumn and winter, and are seen mainly along the River Sorn between its mouth at Bridgend and through the woods as far as the Woollen Mill. They have also been seen on the River Laggan at Island House, and at one or two freshwater lochs, including Lochs Allan and Ballygrant. It was possibly more common in the past and is reported to have bred at some date prior to 1953.

Grey Wagtail *Motacilla cinerea* - a first-year bird feeding in a burn

There are breeding pairs along most of the rivers and burns throughout the island with perhaps 50–100 pairs in all. Many depart south for the winter, and have actually been seen setting off for Ireland from the Oa. They leave behind scattered singles and pairs which, as well as staying beside running water, are often found feeding around freshwater lochs and also along the shore.

Waxwing *Bombycilla garrulus* - a flock looking for more berries

As everywhere in Britain, occurrences on the island are erratic and in greatly varying numbers. In some autumns, just one or two are seen, in others none. However, in major irruption years, as in 2004, there were flocks of 30 or more. As usual, the birds are normally quite tame and feed in gardens where berried shrubs are available taking no notice of people nearby.

Dipper *Cinclus cinclus* - beside a burn

There is a small population of between 10 and 20 pairs, breeding along the rivers and larger burns. Occasional reports from little-visited areas suggest it is probably under-recorded, while its presence at some better-known sites varies from year to year. Most records come from the River Sorn, though this is doubtless linked to the presence of well-walked paths following its course through Bridgend Woods between the village and the wool mill.

Meadow Pipit *Anthus pratensis* - in heather moorland

This is a very widespread and abundant breeding species found over most kinds of open ground, including moorland, rough pastures and dunes. In winter, feeding flocks of up to 100 or so move to the farmland, particularly on stubbles and other harvested crops, as well as to the foreshore and even the roadsides. From sample surveys, it is likely that the island population is at least 5,000 pairs, and quite probably as many as 7,000.

Blackbird *Turdus merula* - a male feasting on rowans

This species is found all over the island wherever there are trees or bushes, so occurs in all types of woodlands, hedges, scrub and gardens. The population has never been estimated but is clearly many hundreds of pairs. There is a marked autumn passage in October and November through the island, with flocks of 50–100, occasionally more, to be seen feeding at the edges of pastures. However, few of these seem to stay for the winter.

Mistle Thrush *Turdus viscivorus* - an adult fluffed up against the cold

Breeding pairs can be found in most of the more mature woodlands on the island, particularly around the edges where these abut on farmland, and also in larger gardens. There are, perhaps, between 50 and 100 pairs in all. Late summer flocks, consisting of up to 15 birds, may be comprised of two or more local families, but slightly larger flocks of up to 25, seen in the autumn, are more likely to be migrants on passage through the island.

Redwing _Turdus iliacus_ - with few rowans left to eat

This is a passage migrant from both Iceland and Scandinavia. From late September, but particularly in the second half of October, thousands, sometimes tens of thousands, are present on the island, often in mixed flocks with Fieldfares. Numbers are very variable from year to year, while onward movement is generally rapid and only a few hundreds stay through the winter. Return passage in March to May is much smaller.

Fieldfare *Turdus pilaris* - with plenty of rowans to eat

Just like the Redwings with which they flock, many thousands, or even tens of thousands, of Fieldfares arrive in October from Scandinavia and stay for the next month or so, gorging on berries or feeding on the shorter pastures. Again, similar to the Redwing, numbers can be very variable and only a few small flocks winter on the island. There is a much smaller return passage in spring.

Collared Dove *Streptopelia decaocto* - a pair sitting in an apple tree

This species first appeared in 1961 with a subsequent rapid increase helped by the amount of spilt grain at the distilleries. Nowadays, although there is reduced grain spill, it is still found in flocks of 20–30 found in some of the villages and in larger gardens.

Turtle Dove *Streptopelia turtur* - an adult shows its neck patch and rufous wing feathers

Single birds, occasionally up to five together, are seen in most summers, the earliest being in April with most records in June to August, and then just a few sightings in September and October. In recent years, it has turned up less frequently than 10–20 years ago.

Treecreeper *Certhia familiaris* - climbing an oak tree

While occurring in all the larger woodlands on the island, both broad-leaved and coniferous, as well as in some larger gardens, this is not a common species and there are probably no more than about 30–40 pairs. It probably increased and has since declined again as the forestry plantations in the Glen matured and then were felled. During the winter, they are occasionally seen in roving flocks of tits.

House Sparrow *Passer domesticus* - an adult male perched typically on a roof
The House Sparrows of Islay appear not to have suffered the major declines reported from elsewhere in the country. They are still widespread around farms and villages, with perhaps 500–1,000 pairs. Although grain is no longer so freely available at every distillery as it once was 20–30 years ago, flocks of up to 100 still occur quite widely, including in farmyards and at well-supplied bird tables.

Raven *Corvus corax* - a wary adult showing off its huge bill

A census in 1997 found about 35 breeding pairs, mostly on sea cliffs, but with some on inland crags or the sides of steep gullies. The refuse disposal tip south of Bowmore is a favourite feeding site for up to 50 or so birds while flocks of 10–20 are often to be seen across the island. After the breeding season, the majority of the island's population roosts in woodland at Bridgend where counts regularly exceed 200, with peaks of over 250.

Looking east over Loch Gruinart

Winter

Great Northern Diver _Gavia immer_ - in winter plumage, with short, thick neck and heavy bill
The largest of the divers, this species is present throughout the autumn and winter in small numbers, especially on Loch Indaal, with mid-winter counts of up to 20, as well as around the coasts in sheltered sea bays such as Claggain, Port Ellen and Sanaig. Between March and May, migrants turn up on Loch Indaal, often peaking at over 150. They are mainly in the outer part of the loch and so can only be seen when the sea is calm.

Slavonian Grebe *Podiceps auritus* - an adult in winter plumage on the sea
A winter visitor arriving in early autumn (September, occasionally August) and staying through until April. Almost all the birds winter on Loch Indaal, especially the inner part between Bowmore and Black Rock, where they build up to a mid-winter peak of up to 50. Their slender black and white forms are usually well spread out across the water, though some can almost always be found close to or among the wintering flock of Scaup.

130

Barnacle Goose *Branta leucopsis* - a mass take-off
The approximately 40,000 Barnacle Geese which arrive in early October and stay well into April represent up to 70% of the total Greenland-breeding population of this species. They feed over most of the farmland, roosting at night principally at the heads of Lochs Gruinart and Indaal. A management scheme compensates the farmers and crofters for the damage they do to the pastures. They are more popular with birdwatchers.

Greenland White-fronted Goose *Anser albifrons flavirostris* **- seven adults coming into land**

Islay is the most important haunt in Britain for this goose. The population numbered around 3–4,000 in the 1960s and 1970s, peaked at about 13,000 in the late 1990s, but has declined to some 8–9,000. This is c.35% of the world population. They arrive in early October and depart in April. They are spread all over the farmland areas of the island, usually in flocks of a few hundreds, sometimes only a few tens.

Lesser Snow Goose *Anser c. caerulescens* - a white-phase adult among Barnacle Geese

One or two are often present during the winter. They can be of either the white or the blue phase and are usually found in flocks of Whitefronts or Barnacles. As they breed in West Greenland in some of the same areas as the Whitefronts, they presumably get caught up in a flock of that species and end up here instead of on the east coast of the USA with the rest of their kind. Sometimes, the same individual has returned to the same part of the island for four or five consecutive winters.

Canada Goose *Branta canadensis* - a 'Lesser' among Barnacle Geese

This species comes to Islay in a variety of sizes. The occasional pair of large birds, similar to those that are widespread in Britain, has attempted to breed but, every winter, up to ten much smaller birds, now called Lesser Canada Geese, turn up in the flocks of Barnacle Geese and, less often, Whitefronts. These are of the types that breed in West Greenland and arctic Canada and are presumed to be vagrants that have strayed across the Atlantic and then found safety among the Barnacles. Some birds return year after year and there have even been two occurrences of birds pairing with a Barnacle Goose and producing hybrid offspring.

Wigeon *Anas penelope* - nine males with just four females

Although mainly a wintering species, occasional birds stay for the summer and one pair bred beside a small pool in 1993. The great majority of the wintering birds are found in Loch Gruinart, up to 750, and in Loch Indaal, where up to 1,000 are present most winters, occasionally 1,500 or more. In the latter loch, they often cluster round up-ending swans and feed on the scraps of *Zostera* grass which they are bringing to the surface.

Green-winged Teal *Anas carolinensis* - a male showing its vertical white stripe
Formerly a subspecies of the Common Teal, but now a species in its own right, it was first reported in 1978. The next sighting was not until the winter of 1996-7, but since then one, occasionally two, males have been seen every winter, almost always on the flooded fields of the RSPB's Loch Gruinart reserve. The regularity with which they can turn up at the same site in succeeding winters suggests returning individuals.

Pintail *Anas acuta* - a male having just taken off

This species used to be quite rare, but the creation in the early 1990s of the flooded marsh at the RSPB's Loch Gruinart reserve encouraged an increase not just there but also at the head of Loch Indaal, the only other regular wintering haunt. Up to 30, occasionally 50 or more, can be seen at both sites between September and April. Pairs lingering into May have brought hopes that they might breed, but this has not yet happened.

Mallard *Anas platyrhynchos* - a male vigorously bathing

A resident species, with breeding pairs found widely on many of the more fertile lochs, but also on tiny farm ponds and flooded ditches. It seems likely there are at least 100 pairs, and possibly quite a lot more. Wintering flocks are found in Loch Gruinart, where there are a regular 200–350, with a peak of over 650, and Loch Indaal, which holds 100–200 and sometimes as many as 400. Smaller numbers are frequent on other wetlands.

136

Red-breasted Merganser *Mergus serrator* - a displaying male

A resident duck, with perhaps 50 pairs breeding around the coasts and up the rivers and beside some of the larger lochs. In late summer, moulting flocks mostly made up of males gather off Blackrock in Loch Indaal, at the south end of Laggan Bay and in Claggain Bay. The flock in Loch Indaal reached over 500 in the early 1990s, so clearly drawing birds from far afield, but is now usually around 100, similar to the other two sites.

Scaup *Aythya marila* - a mixed flock of adult males and females and immatures
The flock of around 1,000 birds, occasionally up to 1,500, wintering in the inner part of Loch Indaal is the second largest flock in Britain. The first birds arrive from their Iceland breeding grounds in August and build up to a December-January peak before declining again, with the last ones staying into May. They are nearly always to be found somewhere between Bowmore and Blackrock and often close inshore.

Long-tailed Duck *Clangula hyemalis* - two males and two females

Most winters there are between five and ten birds present, occasionally more, and nearly always on Loch Indaal, where they can be seen towards the head of the loch, between Bowmore and Blackrock. The first ones arrive in October and one or two may linger into May. There are only a handful of records away from Loch Indaal, usually on the sea, for example offshore of the Rinns at Sanaig, Saligo and passing Frenchman's Rocks.

Goosander *Mergus merganser* - a male - much whiter than the Red-breasted Merganser
There are a small but increasing number of sightings every year, probably related to their spread on mainland Argyll. From one to five birds usually appear sometime between September and April, usually on one or two freshwater lochs, most regularly Ardnahoe, near Bunnahabhain, where the salmon cage may be an attraction. There have also been a few sightings in Loch Indaal.

Goldeneye *Bucephala clangula* - a male about to display to his mate

Small numbers, usually less than ten, occur on many of the more fertile lowland lochs, for example Ardnave, Ballygrant, Finlaggan, Gorm and Skerrols, throughout the winter months. However, the largest numbers are on the sea, particularly in Port Ellen Bay, where up to 40 are regular, while a further 20, occasionally more, can be found in the inner part of Loch Indaal between Bowmore and Blackrock.

142

Greenshank *Tringa nebularia* - an adult in winter plumage
This species has never been found breeding on Islay, which it does further north in Scotland. And although birds are present throughout the year, they remain on the shores of Lochs Gruinart and Indaal and have not been observed even hinting at display in the spring. Three or four birds at a time are regular in both lochs, occasionally a few more, but they are normally solitary or at most in twos and threes.

Grey Plover *Pluvialis squatarola* - almost moulted into winter plumage
Although it can be seen in any month of the year, almost always in Loch Gruinart or Loch Indaal, this is principally an autumn passage migrant with small flocks of 10–20, rarely up to 50–70, regular during August to October. At other times of year, their appearance is more erratic, with ones and twos, less often up to ten together, turning up sometimes just for a few days, though occasionally staying for several weeks.

Purple Sandpiper *Calidris maritima* - an adult in winter plumage on a barnacle-covered rock
This species arrives at the end of October and, in most years, is last seen towards the end of April. Occasional sightings in May are possibly migrants from further south. There are three very traditional wintering sites, around Bowmore harbour, on the rocks in front of Bruichladdich distillery and in the Portnahaven area, each of which holds between 10 and 15 birds, occasionally over 20. It is uncommon elsewhere.

Turnstone *Arenaria interpres* - two winter plumage adults with flecks of summer plumage in their wings
Often seen with Purple Sandpipers, these are regular winter visitors in both Loch Gruinart and Loch Indaal, with up to 100 or more in the former loch and between 50 and 70 in the latter. They prefer rocky and stony shores and are also found in that habitat in smaller numbers around the coasts, including at Ardnave, Claddach, Claggain and Portnahaven. Late stayers in the spring may attain summer plumage before they depart.

Coot *Fulica atra* - feeding on weed
A regular breeder 40 years ago, with wintering flocks exceeding 100, but now a casual winter visitor on, for example, Lochs Ballygrant, Lossit and Skerrols. There has never been a good explanation for the rapid decline and loss as a breeding species.

Moorhen *Gallinula chloropus* - a feeding adult
A relatively uncommon species given the extent of wetland habitat. It is found in marshy pools and large drainage ditches, as well as on fertile lochs, but often just one or two pairs at any one site. The population may only be a few tens of pairs.

Pheasant *Phasianus colchicus* - an adult male in all his glory

This species owes its presence here entirely to releases for shooting which began in the 19th century. Young birds are reared in pens on most of the larger estates, before being released in the late summer. Birds which avoid being shot during their first winter settle down and join the widespread population found in almost all the woodland and scrub areas of the island, feeding out on adjacent farmland and moorland.

Iceland Gull *Larus glaucoides* - in its third winter

From one to three single birds, occasionally more, occur most winters, usually on the coast, for example, in Loch Indaal, at Port Ellen or at Bunnahabhain, but sometimes feeding inland. The majority of records are between September and March but occasional birds stay into May or appear in July and August.

Glaucous Gull *Larus hyperboreus* - in its second winter

This species used to be commoner than the Iceland Gull, with up to five birds most winters but, recently, it has turned up a little less often, but in much the same places as that species. The occasional immature bird has summered.

Great Black-backed Gull *Larus marinus* - an adult showing its heavy bill

Pairs breed all round the coasts usually close to colonies of seabirds on the cliffs, of which they are a major predator. A count in 2000 found a minimum of nearly 60 pairs. During the winter, they roam widely over the island, scavenging where they can and in particular at the refuse disposal tip south of Bowmore, where up to 50 can sometimes be seen.

Rock Dove *Columba livia* - the white rumps confirm they are genuine wild birds

There are several hundred pairs breeding on the island, in coastal caves and in ruined buildings, sometimes with tens of pairs in the one site. Flocks numbering one or two hundred can be seen during the winter, especially on stubble fields. Unlike in many parts of their range, the Islay Rock Doves appear to be true wild birds, with little or no sign of interbreeding with the domesticated form familiar as homing or town centre pigeons.

Barn Owl *Tyto alba* - hunting at night from a perch

With its plentiful rough pastures and woodland, Islay supports a very healthy population of at least 25 pairs. The majority of them breed in the roof spaces of farm buildings and abandoned cottages, although natural holes are also used, including coastal caves and hollow trees. At sites where buildings have either fallen down or been renovated, the provision of nest boxes has proved successful.

Rock Pipit *Anthus spinoletta* - an adult on a lichen-covered boulder

Almost everywhere one goes around Islay's shores, Rock Pipits will be there. Although they favour rocky shores, they will also be found feeding on tidewrack along sandy beaches. The only survey was in 1994 when a minimum 115 pairs were found around part of the coast of the Rinns, not including the cliffs. This would suggest an island population of several hundred pairs.

Great Tit *Parus major* - a male showing its broad breast band

Although found in most of the broad-leaved woodlands and larger gardens, the probable total of 75–100 pairs means that this species is less common than either the Coal or Blue Tits. Winter flocks are uncommon and rarely exceed 10 birds.

153

Blue Tit *Parus caeruleus* - an adult perched on dead nettle stems

Occurs in the same habitats as the Great Tit, but is more numerous with an island population of perhaps 150–250 pairs. Roving autumn and winter flocks of up to 20 are often encountered in the larger woodlands and is, of course, common at bird tables.

154

Starling *Sturnus vulgaris* - an adult in its spotted winter plumage
A widespread and common species, with a breeding population of perhaps 1,000–2,000 pairs. Late summer roosts, often of several hundred birds, form at a number of sites, including the piers at Bruichladdich and Port Ellen and in some of the villages. Additional birds arrive in autumn to spend the winter. Flocks of several hundred birds, sometimes over a thousand, can be seen throughout the winter feeding in the pastures.

**Chaffinch *Fringilla coelebs* - a male regaining
its breeding plumage**

This is a widespread and common breeding species throughout the island, with perhaps 750–1,000 pairs. They are found everywhere where there are trees and bushes, including gardens. During the winter, large flocks of two or three hundred gather on stubble fields and other arable where there is an abundance of weed seeds, and often in mixed flocks with other seed-eating species. There is some passage through the island in autumn.

**Brambling *Fringilla montifringilla* - a male in
winter plumage**

Small numbers (usually less than five, but occasionally 20–30) arrive each autumn in October or November and often stay through the winter. They are most usually seen in flocks of other finches, especially Chaffinches, but sometimes on their own, especially in woodland, for example at Ballygrant and Bridgend.

**Greenfinch *Carduelis chloris* - a male, with a
conspicuous yellow panel on its wings**
A widely if thinly distributed species across the island, with perhaps
50–100 pairs in woodland, scrub and gardens. In the winter, they
come readily to bird tables, and flocks of 30–50, often with other
finches, feed on stubbles and weedy arable fields.

**Siskin *Carduelis spinus* - a male, its black cap
constrasting with its yellow face**
This species probably bred for the first time on Islay in 1972, since
when it has colonised the larger woodlands and conifer plantations
with a current population perhaps approaching 100 pairs. Flocks
can be encountered in winter woodland in winter.

Robin *Erithacus rubecula* - feeding on hawthorn berries

A widespread bird of woodlands of all types, including shelter belts and small copses, as well as scrub and gardens. An island population of 400–500 pairs seems possible. There is some evidence of autumn passage, with loose flocks of up to 20 being seen in October in a number of years at the same time that thrushes were on the move. Twelve together at the Rinns Lighthouse in April one year suggest a small spring migration, too.

Snow Bunting *Plectrophenax nivalis* - in winter plumage

A regular winter visitor in small numbers, with occasional larger flocks. Small numbers of birds, usually less than five, are regular at one or two sites, for example Ardnave and Machir Bay. Larger flocks, mostly of 20–30, but of over 60 in winter 2005-6, turn up from time to time, sometimes to feed on autumn stubbles and then to move on, but in other years staying for longer periods.

Index of photographs

Hen Harrier *Circus cyaneus* - an adult female towards the end of the breeding season
This bird was feeding four well-grown young in a nest on the Rinns. During the summer, her plumage has become worn and pale and she has already begun the annual moult of all her feathers which will last for several more weeks. She has started by moulting some of her wing feathers, producing the obvious gap where two or three inner primaries have been shed and the new ones have not yet appeared.